T0068188

FEAR IS NOT FOR YOU

Step Away From Torment

ESSIE CROCKOM ROBERTS

authorHOUSE®

AuthorHouse™
1663 Liberty Drive
Bloomington, IN 47403
www.authorhouse.com
Phone: 833-262-8899

Published by AuthorHouse 05/21/2021

ISBN: 978-1-6655-2654-8 (sc)
ISBN: 978-1-6655-2653-1 (e)

Library of Congress Control Number: 2021910145

Print information available on the last page.

Scripture quotations marked KJV are from the Holy Bible, King James Version (Authorized Version). First published in 1611. Quoted from the KJV Classic Reference Bible, Copyright © 1983 by The Zondervan Corporation.

This book is printed on acid-free paper.

INTRODUCTION

**The fear of the LORD is a fountain of
life, to depart from the snares of death.**
Proverbs 14:27

His splendor, majesty, might, dominion, power, and authority will rein forever.

Expect God to do the impossible in your life, allow His wisdom to enter your heart, let His knowledge be pleasant to your soul, discretion shall preserve you and understanding will keep you, to deliver you from the way of the evil ones.

We are to respect, reverence and honor God at all times, but have fear of man at no time. Fear God, and keep His commandments. The aggression of an imaginative mind can cause false patterns of belief to become prominent thoughts. This can bring a life filled with a burdensome and boring existence.

**For God hath not given us the spirit of
fear; but of power, and of love, and of a
sound mind. 2 Timothy 1:7.**

Fear comes with torment, infliction of some type of torture of the mind. Following some erroneous doctrine will eventually lead to unfruitfulness and cancel out your true identity as a believer. When God placed Adam and Eve in the garden, they were not suppose to be afraid, they were to obey God.

Genesis 3:9 -10, and the LORD God called unto Adam, and said unto him, where art thou? And he said, I heard thy voice in the garden, and I was afraid, because I was naked; and I hid myself. And He said, who told thee that thou was naked?

ESSIE CROCKOM ROBERTS

MORE RESOURCES
FROM
ESSIE CROCKOM
ROBERTS

GOD'S REPOSITION TO POSITION

Reading this book will encourage the believer to keep an open ear to the voice of the Spirit of the LORD, it's designed to lead you into all truths. Be willing to go all the way, with The Lord.

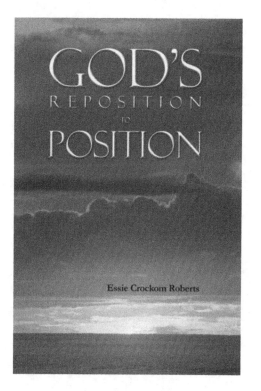

essrob@comcast.net

YONDER WONDERS

Life Changing Revelations

Reading this book will help you polish your life with the newness and freshness of the Holy Spirit within you. This book was written under the leading and guidance of the Holy Spirit. The intent is to inspire the reader not to stop in midair on your way to purpose, nor give up on the call of God for your life.

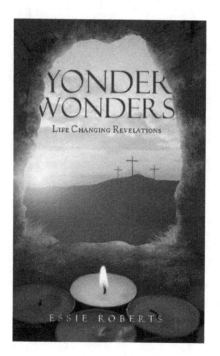

essrob@comcast.net

At some point or time you may have taken possession of a spirit that was not given to you by God, somehow you just took ownership of it. It began to manifest in your body as some type of illness or disease. The truth is, it is really fear that has become inflamed in your body. The inflammation requires a position within the flesh, the flesh is warring against the your spirit. Fear can be accompanied by sickness, which has absolutely nothing to do with the abundant life care package that is part of your inheritance.

For God has not given us the spirit of fear; but of power, and of love, and of a sound mind.
2 TIMOTHY 1:7

God has given you enough grace to remain who He created you to be.

We can no longer try to fashion God to fit or be suitable for our convenience.

He can take us places that our imagination will never be able to match up against.

He is Absolute and Sovereign.

And He said unto me, My grace is sufficient for thee: for my strength is made prefect in weakness.
2 CORINTHIANS 12:9

We so often walk in self-deception, denying His power, using some small minded, unfounded, falsehood that leads to wreckage in life, caused by fear.

Blessed are ye, when men shall revile you, and persecute you, and shall say all manner of evil against you falsely, for my sake.
MATTHEW 5:11

Take the positive tools of your mind from the shelf,
sharpen them with the word of God, and go to a higher level
in your thinking.
Walk away from negative speaking and troubled mined people,
Say good bye, leave negativity in the rear forever.

**Peace I leave with you, my peace I give unto you:
not as the world giveth, give I unto you. Let not
your heart be troubled, neither let it be afraid.
JOHN 14:27**

ESSIE CROCKOM ROBERTS

The body can be inflamed with the spirit of fear.
People suffer from having a spirit of fear,
when carried for an extended period of time.
The body itself become inflamed and suffer unexplainable sickness
which sometimes can not be diagnosed
Let not your heart be trouble any longer.

**He sent His word, and healed them,
and delivered them from
their destructions
PSALM 107:20**

What you believe in your heart is what you will react to, whether good or bad. Following your feeling can cause you to participate in a pity party of one, entertaining yourself, by allowing you and your feelings to be the only guests attending the party.

Believe in the LORD your God, so shall ye be established; believe His Prophet so shall ye prosper.
2 CHRONICLES 20:20

ESSIE CROCKOM ROBERTS

Torment is the Constance companion of fear, it is negative spirits seeking to creep into your thought pattern, which can cause unsound and ineffective judgment under pressure.

There is no fear in love; but prefect love
casteth out fear: because fear has torment. He
that feareth is not made prefect in love.
1 JOHN 4:18

There might be a room in your spiritual living quarters that is furnished with fear, that room must be refurnished and rebuild with faith, faith in the power of the Almighty God.

All scripture is given by inspiration of God, and is profitable for doctrine, for reproof, for correction, for instruction in righteousness. That the man of God maybe perfect, thoroughly furnished unto all Good works 2 TIMOTHY 3:16-17

ESSIE CROCKOM ROBERTS

You can believe and have confident in His ability to make all things work for your good. His power is greater than any accusation, rejection, or intimidating forces ever, for He said that He would never leave you nor forsake you.

Submit yourselves therefore to God. Resist the devil, and he will flee from you.
JAMES 4: 7

Layers of fear can be concealed in unrecognized closets. Closets where the enemy love to hide in dark corners. He can attack you in the loss of a job, business, illness, finances and so much more. He want to control your life by using these layers of fear.

......When the enemy shall comes in like a flood, the Spirit of the LORD shall lift up a standard against him.
ISAIAH 59:19

ESSIE CROCKOM ROBERTS

God's power is always on display. The children of God must strive to fly above the complexities of life, seeing God before us and whatever is in the past, behind us. Try hard not to get impatient, becoming restless can fight your God given promises. Focus on the march to victory.

Fear not, little flock; for it is your Father's good pleasure to give you the kingdom.
LUKE 12:32

If at any time you should feel ill in your body, you must not agree with that illness. You must disagree, by saying with your mouth, by Jesus stripes I am healed. Your body can then come into alignment with what you say with your mouth, at that time healing can began to take place. With the words you confess with your mouth you must be prepared to receive the outcome of those words.

When the even was come, they brought unto him many that were possessed with devils: and He cast out the spirits with His word, and healed all that were sick: MATTHEWS 8:16

ESSIE CROCKOM ROBERTS

Remember when life become most difficult, do not allow fear to be your end, instead let fear be your beginning. Fear the Lord only, it is then that God's truth can be rooted deeper into your life in order to produce richer fruit.

The fear of the LORD is the beginning of wisdom: a good understanding have all they that do His commandments: His praise endureth forever.
PSALM 111:10

God can use the broken pieces of your life to promote you in in the kingdom. Keep in mind, it is the one that the enemy fights the most that has the greatest gift. Don't die in your pain, you were designed to be delivered through your pain.

For He has delivered me out of all trouble: and my eye hath seen His desire upon mine enemies
PSALMS 54:7

Over a period of time life can become loaded with unusable equipment. We can become weighted down with hate, pride, anger, jealousy and other weights of the world. We must instead wear the full armour of God.

Put on the whole armour of God, that ye maybe able to stand against the wiles of the devil. For we wrestle not against flesh and blood, but against principalities, against powers, against the rulers of the darkness of this world, against spiritual wickedness in high places.
EPHESIANS 6: 11-12

Get your love walk in order, all your fears will vanish away.

**There is no fear in love; but perfect love casteth
out fear: because fear hath torment. He that
feareth is not made perfect in love.
1 JOHN 4:18**

Though you may sometime walk through a dark place of despondent, He is always with you. Spiritual development always results in victory.

Yea, though I walk through the valley of the shadow of death, I will fear no evil: for thou art with me; thy rod and thy staff they comfort me.
PSALM 23:4

When going through seasons of darkness, especially where you don't understand what God is doing in your life. Be it known that, He is developing you to be emerged in the likeness of His light.

**In all thy ways acknowledge Him, and He shall direct thy paths. Be not wise in thy own eyes: fear the LORD, and depart from evil.
PROVERBS 3: 6-7**

Rejection is directly related to the call of God on your life. Remember Jesus Himself was rejected by men.

So that we my boldly say, the LORD is my helper and I will not fear what man shall do unto me.
HEBREWS 13:6

In the area that the enemy attacks you the most, causing you to fear, God wants to give you, your greatest achievement, your greatest break through.

Though an host should encamp against me, my heart shall not fear: though war should rise up against, in this will be confident. One thing have I desired of the LORD, that will seek after; that I may dwell in the house of the LORD. all the days of my life, to behold the beauty of the LORD, and to inquire in His temple.
PSALM 27:3-4

See the mighty hand of the LORD leading you through the healing fields, touching your body as you trust Him to deliver you from every hindering force. Go over the mountain cross the bridge, open the gate, go into the fields and rest in His care.

But he saith unto them, it is I; be not afraid.
JOHN 6:20

A large number of people can't seem to find time to fit God into their day,
but they are constantly wanting God to fix their day,
He is the one who created man and the day.
It would be wise to acknowledge Him as LORD at the beginning of each day, not having fear of any day.

What time I am afraid, I will trust in thee. In God I will praise His word, in God I will put my trust; I will not fear what flesh can do unto me.
PLSAM 56:3-4

ESSIE CROCKOM ROBERTS

A drifting mind is planted by the enemy in order to cause distraction, keeping your focus away from the loving Father, who truly want to be the one to order your steps.

Thou will keep him in prefect peace, whose mind is stayed on thee: because he trusteth in thee. Trust ye in the LORD for ever: for in the LORD JEHOVAH is everlasting strength:
ISAIAH 26:3-4

There can be a war on the inside of you, but so are the weapons of your war fare within you. You must realize that there are also great weapons which have been place on the inside of you by the Holy Spirit, where by every battle can be won.

The thief cometh not, but for to steal, and to kill, and to destroy: I am come that they might have life, and that they might have it more abundantly.
JOHN 10:10

Every answer we need is in the hand of the King. Draw near to Him,
He will draw near to you. God is the solution to your problems

**Fear not, little flock; for it is your Father's
good pleasure to give you the kingdom.
LUKE 12:32**

Sometimes we are not as strong as we think, but we are also not as week as we think.

God preserve and build us upon the eternal blessed hope of His calling.

He has released us from the spirit of bondage and fear.

**For ye have not received the spirit of bondage
again to fear; but ye have received
the spirit of adoption, whereby we cry Abba Father
ROMANS 8:15**

The Holy Spirit can show you places in your heart where He can not enter because of your own accumulation of fragments of fear that is embedded firmly in rock solid places of your heart. The way out is to ask The Father to lead you in clearing a path for His Spirit to flow through.

And there shall come a forth a rod out of the stem of Jesse, and a Branch shall grow out of His roots. And the spirit of the LORD shall rest upon Him, the spirit of wisdom and understanding, the spirit of counsel and might, the spirit of knowledge of the fear of the LORD.
ISAIAH 11:1-2

Fear is the opposite of faith. Reject fear and embrace faith. Fear will take flight when it sees faith approaching.

**And immediately Jesus stretched forth His hand,
and caught him, and said unto him, O thou
of little faith, wherefore didst thou doubt?
MATTHEW 14:31**

We overcome by the blood of the Lamb, and the words of our testimony. There is a miracle in your mouth, resist the voice of the enemy and speak the word of the LORD.

**Submit yourselves therefore to God. Resist
the devil, and he will flee from you.
Draw nigh to God, and He will draw nigh to you......
JAMES 4: 7-8**

You are a servant of God, who walk in His authority, which put you in position to score. The enemy is trying to guard you, trying his best to hold you back from making it to home plate.

**The LORD is my light and my salvation;
whom shall I fear? The LORD is the strength
of my life; of whom shall I be afraid?
PSALM 27:1**

ESSIE CROCKOM ROBERTS

The enemy's weapon against you is dismantled by the Holy Spirit. God has conquered all your enemies, put your trust in Him. The battle is over. You win!

These things I have spoken unto you, that
in me ye might have peace. In the world
ye might have tribulations: but be of good
cheer; I have overcome the world.
JOHN 16:33

God's love for you and I will never change. He is the Master Lover. See all things from His prospective. He can do the impossible.

The secret of the LORD is with them that fear Him; and He will show them His covenant.
PSALM 25: 14

ESSIE CROCKOM ROBERTS

There is a work to be done, it is call kingdom work, setting the captive free.

Speak the word of God boldly and plainly without hesitation.

There is absolutely no time or place for fear to be on display.

In God I will praise His word, in God I will put my trust; I will not fear what flesh can do unto to me.
PSALM 56:4

Step away from strife and confusion, stay clear. It is a holding cell for your spirit, you must choose to fly above the complexities of life.

Having therefore these promises, dearly beloved, let us cleanse ourselves from all filthiness of the flesh and spirit, perfecting holiness in the fear of the God.
2 CORINTHIANS 7:1

Carry Christ closer than any pain you may encounter. He has the inexhaustible energy to get you through it all.

**Ye shall not fear them: for the LORD
your God, He shall fight for you.
DEUTERONOMY 3:22**

The word of God must be the driving force in your life in helping you to relinquish all sin. He take pleasure in those that fear Him.

**For great is the LORD, and greatly to
be praised: He is also to be feared
above all gods
1 CHRONICLES 16:25**

ESSIE CROCKOM ROBERTS

Look not for a one time event with the LORD, but seek for the process of doing His will. Stay with the processor. God is your protector, for you have nothing to fear.

Yea, though I walk through the valley of the shadow of death, I will fear no evil: for thy art with me; thy rod and thy staff they comfort me.
PSALM 23:4

When you face hardship, opposition or adversity, you can still have hope because God is a constant present companion, with His love comes an intimate relationship.

**The LORD is on my side; I will not
fear: what can man do unto me?
PSALM 118:6**

ESSIE CROCKOM ROBERTS

The void places in life can bring about the fear of loneliness. God has the power to set your feet upon a solid rock and establish all of your goings.

What time I am afraid, I will trust in Thee.
PSALM 56:3

God has not designed His elect to be stuck behind walls of discouragement, disappointment, shame or especially confusion. His power will bring you from behind the enemy's walls of fear.

Thou shall not be afraid for the terror by night; not for the arrows that flieth by day
PSALM 91:5

ESSIE CROCKOM ROBERTS

Do not make it a habit of praying begging prayers. Pray prayers of thanksgiving, speaking the word of God in your prayers. The word can change circumstances and create a freshness and a newness in your life. Release your faith by using your mouth to confess His word.

Therefore I say unto you, what things so ever ye desire, when ye pray believe that ye receive them, and ye shall have them.
MARK 11:24

The written word is so much more than ink on paper, it is the word of God speaking to those who can receive and believe the very articulation of it all.

He shall not be afraid of evil tidings: his
heart is fixed, trusting in the LORD. His
heart is established, he shall not be afraid,
until he see his desire upon his enemies.
PSALM 112:7 & 8

Living a life controlled by fear will contaminate life's plans, thus you may never really know what the LORD had in store for you.

For I know the thoughts that I think toward you, saith the LORD, thoughts of peace, and not of evil, to give you an expected end.
JEREMIAH 29:11

The entanglement of guilt and shame were all left at the cross, where it was crucified with Christ. Rest assured, He is in the mist of all that concerns you.

Stand fast therefore in the liberty wherewith Christ hath made us free, and be not entangled again with the yoke of bondage
GALATIANS 5:1

Yea,
PS :4

44   ESSIE CROCKOM ROBERTS

The circumstances on earth has no ownership over you. Your freedom has been purchased with the blood of Jesus Christ.

Fret not thyself because of evildoers, neither by thou envious against the workers of iniquity. For they will soon be cut down like the grass, and wither as the green herb.
PSALM 37: 1-2

Fear will keep your expectations of God from making good on His promises at a very low scale. He has promise to never leave you nor forsake you.

Be not afraid of their faces: for I am with thee to deliver thee, saith the LORD.
JEREMIAH 1:8

Remember there is the rock that is bigger than you are and so much stronger than you are. He is the person of the Holy Spirit. When you do your very best, He will flatten the opposition. The only fear we should encounter is the fear of God.

By mercy and truth iniquity is purged: and by the fear of the LORD men depart from evil.
PROVERBS 16:6

When your heart is right, your feet will find a way to follow. Let your expectations be from God.

Having therefore these promises, dearly beloved, let us cleanse ourselves from all filthiness of the flesh and spirit, perfecting holiness in the fear of the God.
2 CORINTHIANS 7:1

It is possible to live so low, coupled with fear, that it become the practice of living beneath your God given privileges. You can become distracted by a life of routine living, which can make it impossible to hear when the Spirit speak.

Peace I leave with you, my peace I give unto you: not as the world giveth, give I unto you. Let not your be troubled, neither let it be afraid.
JOHN 14:27

Overcoming fear began its development when planting the seed of the word of God in the soil of your heart. Good seed sown in fresh soil, watered daily can produce confident in what you are expecting to manifest in garden of your life.

Now the parable is this: The seed is the word of God.
LUKE 8:11

You have no battles to fight, every battle have been fought and won for you.

Whatever you are looking for, searching for, you already have it. God had the solution before you had the problem.

And the LORD, He it is that doth go before thee; He will be with thee, He will not fail thee, neither forsake thee: fear not, neither be dismayed.
DEUTERONOMONY 31:8

Amazingly in the scripture, God places the ones who are fearful in the same category with a very powerful group of other sins.

But the fearful, and unbelieving, and the abominable, and murderers, and whoremongers, and sorcerers, and idolaters, and all liars, shall have their part in the lake which burneth with fire and brimstone: which is the second death.
REVELATION 21:8

It pays to consult with what is in your Holy Spirit benefit package, recognize what is bestowed to you. Know that it is beyond man's scrutiny.

Do not permit yourself to be fearful, intimidated or cowardly unsettled.

Fret not thyself because of evildoers, neither be thou envious against the workers of iniquity. For they shall soon be cut down like the grass, and wither as the green herb.
PSALM 37:1-2

You are not chiseled out from some stone. God Himself created you. Why should you allow some sculptor of a man to try and recreate God' master piece? We live and move and have our being in God.

**In God have I put my trust: I will not be
afraid what man can do unto me.
PSALM 56:11**

Afraid To engage in something new or different? Remember your life's journey is with the LORD. His mercies are new every morning.

…..Why are you fearful, Oh ye of little faith?….
MATTHEW 8:26

The Spirit of the LORD that is within you is like a compass. It will always point you in the way of the LORD at any given time.

**But straightway Jesus spake unto them saying,
be of good cheer; it is I; be not afraid.
MATTHEW 14:27**

ESSIE CROCKOM ROBERTS

Confidence in the Father will drive away fear and anxiety whereby giving you His peace.

**Ye shall not need to fight in this battle:
set yourselves, stand ye still, and see the
salvation of the LORD with you,......
2 CHRONICLES 20:17**

God encourages us to deepen our relationship with Him, to allow a more intimate relationship to develop. Fear of man can never be a part of this equation.

**The fear of the LORD is the beginning of wisdom:
and the knowledge of the Holy is understanding.
PROVERBS 9:10**

Undercover fear, is in direct proportion to hidden fear. Putting on a brave face when there is absolutely no faith in God to handle whatever the situation may be. Not trusting God becomes hard to keep fear a secret.

Peace is then absent from your life.

Fear them not therefore: for there is nothing covered, that shall not be revealed; and hid, that shall not be known.
MATTHEW 10:26

Get equipped to go into the enemy's camp and take back your stuff. Began to speak the appropriate word of God that shuts down all fear.

A man has joy by the answer of his mouth: and a word spoken in due season, how good is it!
PROVERBS 15:23

ESSIE CROCKOM ROBERTS

When the enemy comes to you with the slightest image of fear, it is at that very moment that you must renounce his voice and work of discouragement. Do not entertain no parts of his method.

His heart is established, he shall not be afraid, until he see his desire upon his enemies. PSALMS 112:8

The running waters of peace, will submerge all fear, bringing peace like a clam river.

**When a man's ways please the LORD, He maketh
even his enemies to be at peace with him.
PPOVERBS 16:7**

Remove your hand from the self-destruct button of fear, allow the peace of God to set you up with an untroubled heart.

The fear of the LORD tendeth to life: and he that hath it shall abide satisfied; he shall not be visited with evil.
PPOVERBS 19:23

When the mind is rapped up in negative, nagging and unproductive thoughts, there will be no peace to abide in. Your forward progress will become a challenged, taunted by your own mind insults

For as he thinketh in his heart, so is he:.......
PPOVERBS 23:7

God has already made you an over comer. Use your overcoming power to gain the superiority over all your fears.

**For whatsoever is born of God overcometh the world:
and this is the victory that overcometh the world,
even our faith. Who is he that overcometh the world,
but he that believeth that Jesus is the son of God?
1 JOHN 5: 4-5**

Faith that swims through layers of fear, can be defined as conquering faith, overcoming obstacles or oppositions, that swims through inflamed fear.

Nay, in all things we are more than conquerors through Him that loved us
ROMANS 8:37

You have a promissory note written especially to you, with an assurance that whatever is trying to drag you down and put you into fear, He has already overcome, no need for you to fear.

Who is he that overcometh the world, but he that believeth that Jesus is the Son of God?
1 JOHN 5: 5

Walking in the peace of God is a priceless tool to process. Reject any fear, make a decision to stay with the peace that God gives, you will never be able to use it all up.

**Endeavouring to keep the unity of the
Spirit in the bond of peace.
EPHESIANS 4: 3**

ESSIE CROCKOM ROBERTS

The word of God helps us to stay anchored in Him so that we can withstand life's storms.

Ask God, where is the good way, then go and walk in it.

**As ye have therefore received Christ Jesus
the LORD, so walk ye in Him.
COLOSSIANS 2:6**

There is nothing more that can prepare you for life's test than a deep knowledge of God's word. The word of God is our foundation, it is immeasurable.

**Now thanks be unto God, which always causeth
us to triumph in Christ, and maketh manifest the
savour of His knowledge by us in every place.
2 CORINTHIANS 2:14**

Taking ownership of the spirit of fear will automatically activate the enemy and his works of darkness. One of his assignments is to fan in flames of fear

**But and if ye suffer for righteousness
sake, happy are ye: and be not afraid of
their terror, neither be troubled;
1 PETER 3:14**

God's love is forever focused on you, it's unconditional and undying. He has always know your destiny. Remember, He calls the shots.

**Greater love has no man than this, that a
man lay down his life for his friends.
JOHN 15:13**

Do not cave into the intimidations of self-pity formed by the complexities of your life.
You were ordained for excellence.

But we have this treasure in earthen vessel, that the excellency of the power maybe of God, and not of us.
2 CORINTHIANS 4:7

Your God given assignment can sometimes magnify your problems. Push and keep pushing pass the fear of every attack, it's only a test of your faith, which will allow you to fully operate in your calling.

And being fully persuaded that, what He had promised, He was able to perform. And therefore it was imputed to him for righteousness.
ROMANS 4:21-22

Fear is cancelled out by faith, faith come by hearing the word of God.

**Thy word have I hid in my heart, that
I might not sin against thee.
PSALM 119:11**

How amazing it is that God will use our inadequacies to fulfill His purpose in us and draw us closer to Him in the process.

But it was good for me to draw near to God:
I have put my trust in the LORD GOD,
that I may declare all thy works.
PSALM 73:28

ESSIE CROCKOM ROBERTS

With God before you, your fears behind you, You can march all the way to victor, commissioned and anointed for His own service.

Now He which stablisheth us with you in Christ, and hath anointed us, is God.
2 CORINTHIANS 1:21

The only fight you will have is the fight of faith, not of fear.
Embrace faith in God and watch all your fears disappear.

**I have fought a good fight, I have finished
my course, I have keep the faith.**
2 TIMOTHY 4:7

Fear not, believe only, raise your expectations, for God has arrested every negative spirit that would try to overpower and overcome who you were fashioned to be.

**Thy hands has made me and fashioned me:
give me understanding, that I may
learn thy commandments.
PSALMS 119:73**

Your imagination can open you up to a continuous state of fear. Being surrounded by fear for so long, that seemingly everything and everybody you encounter will carry some type of a fear factor for you.

There were they in great fear, where no
fear was: for God hath scattered the bones
of him that encampeth against thee:
PSALMS 53:5

When a spirit of fear attach itself to you, you are headed for a major defeat unless you know how to swim to the other side where faith in God awaits you.

**He shall not be afraid of evil tidings: his
heart is fixed, trusting in the LORD.
PSALMS 112:7**

When a spirit of fear become evident, we must immediately rely on the help of the HOLY SPIRIT to protect our emotions, and trust Him to spring up the wells of comfort and strength.

He giveth power to the faint; and to them that have no might He increaseth strength.
ISAIAH 40:29

A fear alarm can be triggered where love is absent. The love walk can be out of step where bitterness is on display. True love expresses the heart of God toward His people.
His love shall never fail.

Greater love has no man than this, that a man lay down his life for his friends
JOHN 15:13

To wear the fear of the LORD is to have search a deep respect for God and His word that you refuse to do anything outside of His will, because of your respect and value for His order of life.

For even hereunto were we called: because Christ also suffered for us, leaving us an example, that ye shall follow His steps:
1 PETER 2:21

The fear of the LORD is the beginning of wisdom. God takes pleasure in those that fear the LORD thy God and serve Him.

**By mercy and truth iniquity is purged: and by the fear of the LORD men depart from evil.
PROVERB. 16:6**

The forces of fears can slip by the unguarded mind of the natural being, man, whereby placing him in confinement of the flesh and bring him into an undesirable prison living in constant fear.

Attend unto my cry; for I am brought very low: deliver me from my persecutors; for they are stronger than I. Bring my soul out of prison, that I my praise thy name: PSALM 142: 6-7

A wicked spirit always walk in fear, for it is constantly worried of being uncovered and exposed by truth. Jesus is the way the truth and the light. Avoid taking the path of the wicked spirit of fear.

The fear of the wicked, it shall come upon him: but the desire of the righteous shall be granted.
PROVERBS 10:24

Do not go in the way of the undesirable, escape the wicked one plans to imprison you with his many levels of compounded fear. Bypass every dark alley before it becomes an invasion of total darkness.

Then Jesus said unto them, yet a little while is the light with you. Walk while you have the light, lest darkness come upon you: for he that walketh in darkness knoweth not whither he goeth.
JOHN 12: 35

Are you afraid to engage in something new or different because of inflamed layers of fear being pressed upon you by the enemy's flooding forces? Over coming fear is a must.

The fear of the LORD prolonged days: but the years of the wicked shall be shortened
PROVERBS 10:27

Anticipation or an awareness of danger can set one up for fear of achievement, Apprehensiveness caused by some great alarm of danger ahead. can bring about total stagnation

But He answered and said, It is written, Man shall not live by bread alone, but by every word that proceeds out of the mouth of God.
MATTHEW 4:4

CONSIDER PRAYING PSALMS 91 EVERYDAY

PSALMS 91

Verses 1-4

He that dwelleth in the secret place of the most High shall
abide under the shadow of the Almighty.
I will say of the LORD, He is my refuge and my fortress:
my God; in Him will I trust.
Surely He shall deliver thee from the snare of the fowler
and from the noisome pestilence.
He shall cover thee with His feathers, and
under His wings shalt thou trust:
His truth shall thy shield and buckler.

PSALMS 91

Verses 5-8

Thou shall not be afraid for the terror by night;
nor for the arrow that flieth by day;
nor for the pestilence that walket in darkness;
nor for the destruction that wasteth at noonday.
A thousand shall fall at thy side, and ten thousand
at thy right hand; but it shall not come night thee.
Only with thine eyes shall thou behold and see the
reward of the wicked.

PSALMS 91

Verses 9-12

Because thou hast made the LORD, which is my refuge,
even the most High, thy habitation.
There shall no evil befall thee, neither shall
any plague come nigh thy dwelling.
For He shall give His angels charge over thee,
to keep thee in all thy ways.
They shall bear thee up in their hands,
lest thou dash thy foot against a stone.

PSALMS 91

Verses 13-16

Thou shall tread upon the lion and the adder:
the young lion and the dragon shall
thou trample under feet.
Because he has set his love upon me,
therefore will I deliver him:
I will set him on high, because he has known my name.
He shall call upon me, and I will answer him:
I will be with him in trouble; I will deliver him,
and honour him. With long life will I satisfy him,
and show him my salvation.

To fear the LORD is the beginning of knowledge: but fools despise wisdom and instruction. Proverbs 1:7

If you say yes to the will of God for your life, you will never have to fear, any thing or any body, for He knows the way you should go. Just say yes, submit and obey. Saying yes is the sure road to advance your purpose in the kingdom of God. Fear is not your task, it was not given to you, it is your enemy. Having restless days and nights, taking your coffee breaks with negative thoughts planted by seeds of fear, is a crippling diseases. The prescription for doing away with fear, is putting ones faith and trust in God. He will keep you from the snares of the workers of iniquities, causing your heart to never be troubled or afraid.

Printed in the United States
by Baker & Taylor Publisher Services

Printed in the United States
by Baker & Taylor Publisher Services